DAILY
REFLE

BY E. JAMES ROHN

BROLGA
PUBLISHING PTY LTD
· A C N 063 962 443 ·

Published by Brolga Publishing PTY LTD ACN 063 962 443
P.O. Box 959, Ringwood, Victoria 3134, Australia

Copyright © E. J. Rohn

All rights reserved. Without limiting the rights under copyright above, no part of this publication may be reproduced, stored into a retrieval system, or transmitted in any form or by any means (electronic, mechanical, photocopying, recording or otherwise), without the prior written permission of both the copyright owner and the publisher.

Design and Production by Pro Art Design, Adelaide.

Printed and bound at Griffin Paperbacks, Australia.

National Library of Australia Cataloguing-in-Publication entry:
ISBN 0-909608-11-3

Disclaimer: Every attempt has been made to identify and contact owners of copyright for permission to reproduce material in this book. However any copyright holders who have inadvertently been omitted from acknowledgements and credits should contact the publishers. Any omissions will be rectified in subsequent editions.

Daily Reflections

Happiness is an art not an accident.

Daily Reflections

Design the joy you want, fashion it like you are weaving a tapestry.

~

It is a basic law of life that demands either human progression or human regression.

Daily Reflections

Don't cheat - it never seems to
work out well.

Sometimes the "why" can change your life.
So - "why not"?

Check results regularly to make sure if you are moving in or moving out.

Daily Reflections

Take full responsibility, you ask the question and you answer the question.

Learn how to live well.

~

If you wish to be wealthy - study wealth.
If you wish to be happy - study happiness.

Daily Reflections

Know how to arrive at any destination.

Daily Reflections

Five major pieces to life's puzzle are:
1. What you know
2. What you feel
3. What you do
4. Check results
5. Lifestyle

We are affected by what we feel.

Start with education not motivation.

Fix what's going on inside and you can change
your life forever.

A miracle is something that we don't understand
how it works. We just know it does.

If you give a child a dollar and let him spend the whole dollar saying, "Well, it's only a dollar and he's only a child," when would you want that attitude to change?
When he's fifty?

Daily Reflections

Result is the name of the game.

~

Do the best you can.

Winter always comes. We are either prepared
or unprepared.

~

If you just do what you can - you'll make a living.
If you do the best you can - you'll make a
fortune.

Daily Reflections

Invest philosophy and attitude
in activity.

Why is a potential mother willing to put herself through what she knows will be a painful experience? Because it is the only way to create new life.

Daily Reflections

Do what you can - it will start a miracle process.

Establish the disciplines that will take you to where you want to go - then do them.

You have to have a good feeling about yourself.

$\smile$

We are affected by the disciplines we take.

Wisdom does nothing on its own. Wisdom must be invested in activity and discipline.

We have to pay the price to get the promise - but the price is easy if the promise is clear.

Daily Reflections

Design the promise and take confident
steps everyday.

⌣

One person doesn't make a symphony orchestra.

You have to have a sense of appreciation for the "all of us" that makes the contribution to "each of us" to change our lives.

Learn from the past, gather up experience.

Daily Reflections

Have the future well planned, well designed.

Don't stumble into tomorrow with apprehension.

Autumn is the season for harvesting the fruits of our springtime labour.

You are deserving - you are becoming - and you shall succeed.

"As you sow, so shall you reap."
Remember what we put into this world, we get back from it.

Call the future - the Promise.

Human character is formed not in the absence of difficulty but in our response to difficulty.

Walk confidently into tomorrow having your promise of the future well planned.

Daily Reflections

The things that are easy to do are also easy
NOT to do.
That's the difference between success and failure.

~

Library cards are free. But in America only 3% of
the population has a library card.

It doesn't matter where you are, opportunities are everywhere.

What you perceive yourself to be, determines the quality of your life.

Smile at adversity but act quickly to eliminate it.

Become a good listener.

Daily Reflections

Sort through all the voices and find the best ones,
and then stick with them.

Stay for a while with voices of value.

There is no substitute for reading.

~

Become self-educated.

Never cease your quest
for knowledge.

Learn where the possibilities are and how to maximise them.

Daily Reflections

Let the university of life teach you everyday.

Learn from life - learn from the day.

Daily Reflections

Most people try to get through the day. I'm asking you to get FROM the day.

Daily Reflections

Keep a journal.
If you see something valuable, hear
something valuable,
or read something valuable,
write it down -
don't leave it to memory.

Daily Reflections

Be a serious student of your own life.

Learn from O.P.E. - Other People's Experience.

Learn from the negatives as well as the positives.

Observe - you've got to watch what's happening.

Pay attention!

Don't miss the tragedy - don't miss
the opportunity.
Don't miss the problem - don't miss the answer.

Daily Reflections

The wind that blows is what brings
us opportunity.

~

Each person's philosophy is like the set of the sail.

Daily Reflections

Don't wish for a better wind - wind blows on us all - learn to set a better sail.

Daily Reflections

Philosophy, the ability to use our mind, is that which makes us different from all other life forms.

Daily Reflections

Look and search for ways and means to let your mind be filled with the ideas and information that can change your life.

The ability to think, to ponder, means we have the ability to change the course of our life.

Daily Reflections

Each person's philosophy is the major determining factor in how their life works out.

Truth is old - there are no new discoveries.

One way to learn to do it right is by doing it wrong.

~

Learn from personal experience.

It's not that things cost too much, it's that you can't afford them.

If you will change - everything will change for you.

Don't care about the wind that blows - rather, be
so ready and so equipped that you can handle
any circumstance.

~

Look what can happen to a farm boy from Idaho
with a few ideas simply put - but
thoroughly executed!

Daily Reflections

In your life there are about half a dozen things that make 80% of the difference.

Keep looking for the few things that make the most difference.

Spend most of your time working on those things
that are going to make the most difference.

The challenge of self-expression is putting into
words what you know and how you feel.

Daily Reflections

Every once in a while take a new look at your life.

So you never miss anything good or valuable -
take notes.

Daily Reflections

Be a searcher, recorder, reviewer of a good idea.

Daily Reflections

Keep trying and you will get better at what you do.

If what you get is the result of an investment, rather than a taking, know that this is what makes society work and the world work.

~

Self-preservation is one of the strongest instincts we have.

When you share an idea you get to hear it again.

If you're given something in return for what you have given - everyone benefits.

There isn't anything more valuable
than the repetition of a good idea.

Ideas heard have one effect. But ideas repeated and spoken, and that grow from conversation, are the ones that have meaning in our life.

Daily Reflections

Share an idea with ten people they get to hear it once but you get to hear it ten times which means you get the best end of the deal.

If something has meaning for you, find a way to share it because the more often you share it the more value you will get from it.

Sincerity is not a test of truth.

It is possible to be sincerely wrong.

Daily Reflections

Better to have a variety of teachers and pick the best from each of them.

The season of Summer is for growing and gaining strength.

Daily Reflections

In order to do well we need Ideas
and Inspiration.

It isn't how much you learn - it's how much you
learn and use.

Without inspiration ideas are stillborn.

Spring is a time for creation of things of value.

Look for the miraculous - hidden among the common.

Daily Reflections

Desperation can be an inspiration.

Daily Reflections

Ideas are as close as your nearest book.
Ideas are as close as your nearest library.

Life is conditional.

Good ideas are as close as the time you take to ponder them.

Ideas are those subtle things that are waiting for people to make the effort to search for them, and unless you make the search they stay undisclosed.

Life is an if:
If you search - you will find.
If you don't search - you won't find.

Life was not designed to respond to need.
Life was designed to respond to condition.

Daily Reflections

The greater the need, the greater the need to meet the condition.

~

Let the obvious be your best teacher.

Daily Reflections

You only have a chance to reap if first you plant.

Life is truly a constant beginning.

Daily Reflections

"If you make a move toward me, I will make a move toward you."
- Old Testament.

If you make a move toward your dream - your dream will make a move toward you.

Daily Reflections

Today's procrastination will surely be tomorrow's regret.

⌣

It's OK to be nobly self-interested.

Daily Reflections

Be faithful over small things.

～

It is OK to be wealthy because of what you become in pursuit of it.

What you become is much more important
than what you get.

What you get is directly related to the
person you become.

Be like an ant, an ant will never quit. Ant's think
winter in the summer and work hard.

Be careful in the summer and don't build
on the sand.

Gather all you possibly can while the sun
is shining.

In the time allotted to labour do the best you can.

Doing less than you can, messes with the mind and deteriorates your life.

It's not the amount that counts, it's the extent of your reach.

Choose a smile - not a frown.

Today adds to yesterday.

Learn to live on 70% of your income.

Teach our kids to be enterprising. Teach them how to invest as well as labour.

Work full-time on your job and part-time on
your fortune.

The essence of springtime is faith woven among
the threads of massive human effort

Philosophy is what you know, and how you
feel about it.

Nothing happens for you until it happens to you.

If we want more we must
become more.

Work harder on yourself than you do on your job.

Wealth is not something you go after - it is something you attract.

Success is not something you pursue - it is something you become.

Promise only comes if you pay the price.

Daily Reflections

Zero in on objectives.

Daily Reflections

Don't give up on your dreams.

Daily Reflections

Set your goals then act on them.

Put your ideas on paper - it is like building a house, you put the plan on paper first.

Daily Reflections

Don't start the day until you have it finished.

∨

Operate from document not from thought.

You are now a seasoned warrior, you bear the scars of honourable battle, and here is where you stand today.

Daily Reflections

Let's do something remarkable!

Be thankful!

Make an actual as well as a conscious mental list, tangible as well as intangible.

Give people the gift of your attention.

Courtesy is contagious.

Daily Reflections

Write at least one thankyou or encouraging letter every week.

Daily Reflections

Draw on all you have learned and practised.

How great to have a mind to expand, and a
soul to nourish.

Develop a growing awareness of the world around
you and your possibility in it.

Facts and faith and action - what a combination for personal progress.

~

Learn to work harder on yourself than anything else.

Daily Reflections

The best answer to worry is confidence. Start with self-confidence.

Daily Reflections

Use daily discipline to achieve.

Daily Reflections

It's not what you can do - it's what you will do.

~

Create your own environment and learn to control it.

Start doing all the things that would make you feel better: exercise, diet, read more.

Life is like a stream that flows continuously.

Daily Reflections

You can only hunt elk when the snow falls in the high mountains and drives them down.

Daily Reflections

Make something out of each opportunity.

Daily Reflections

Don't be afraid to face the winter of life,
remembering spring always follows.

Help me to see it as it is.
Help me to see it better than it is,
and then inspire me to act.

Worry is just fear painting pictures in your mind.

Worry left unchecked can become like a mad dog loose in the house.

Use worry instead of letting worry use you.

Let fear advise you of the facts but never let fear determine your reactions.

Believe your beliefs,
then practise them.

Confidence starts first with awareness.

Life and business are like the changing seasons.

Learn how to handle the winter and take advantage of the spring.

Worry is the number one killer of dreams, achievement, energy and vitality.

Work your way past the mine fields of worry and disaster, and out into the clear air of mental sunshine.

If I did it - anybody can.

Don't ask for the task to be easy, ask for it to be worth it.

Don't wish it were easier, wish you were better.

Don't ask for less problems, ask for more wisdom.

If you wish away your experiences you wish your life away.

~

Miss a meal if you have to, but don't miss a book.

Daily Reflections

My father taught me to always do more than you get paid for as an investment in your future.

~

It's not the amount that counts - it is the plan and what you do with it.

Daily Reflections

Poor people spend their money and save
what is left.
Rich people save their money and spend
what is left.

⌣

Don't just learn how to earn, learn how to live.

A few treasures are better than a houseful of junk.

Friends: Ask yourself, who do I spend time with and what do they do to me?

Daily Reflections

If you are faithful over a few things you will be
made ruler over many.

∨

Find people of substance and spend more time
with them.

Take good care of your body, it's the only place you have to live.

Those who seek a better life must first become a better person.

It is the small disciplines that lead to the great accomplishments.

All disciplines affect each other. Everything affects everything else.

Keep looking for the small disciplines
that will cause us to refine our
thinking, amend our errors,
and improve our results.

The journey towards the good life begins with a serious commitment to changing any aspect of our current philosophy that has the capacity to come between us and our dreams.

How effectively we use the present is largely
determined by our attitude to the past.

Our better future begins in the current moment.

Whatever the mind has the capacity to imagine,
it also has the ability to create.

Why are we always ready to applaud someone
else's accomplishment - and yet so shy about
recognising our own?

Human beings with limited knowledge lack the "mental colours" with which to create a complete picture.

We are the only ones who can do the special
things we do. And what we do is special.

⌣

Our attitude is an asset, a treasure of great value
which must be protected.

Beware the vandals and thieves who would injure our positive attitude or seek to steal it away.

~

It is our responsibility to do something with whatever life has handed us.

Take all that you have and all that you are -
and put it to work.

Demonstrate on the outside all of the value you
possess on the inside.

Affirmations are important. But affirmations without discipline are the beginnings of delusion.

~

As Shakespeare observed, "The fault...is not in the stars, but in ourselves."

Dream about the future then design it.

~

Start with yourself - with the development of new disciplines.

Daily Reflections

Success really starts by becoming master over the
small details of our lives.

All the great rewards in life are available
to each of us.

Daily Reflections

Ponder all that is possible.

Results are the harvest that comes from
our past efforts.

Opportunity merely presents itself - it does not pause or linger.

Use past lessons to serve you - not to overwhelm you.

Now is the time to fix the future.

∨

Life gets better when we get better.

Having more doesn't make us more. It merely magnifies what we already are.

Acquire more value - not more valuables.

Difficulty tests the strength of our resolve.

⌣

Results respond to effort, labour and activity.

A tree does not grow to half of its
potential size and then say,
"I guess that will do."
How about you?

We don't have to be rich to live richly. The admission price to a fabulous sunset is free!

Begin this very day, the process of creating experiences and memories that will endure in the hearts of those you love, long after you are gone.

We are the sum total of all those people and events that have touched us since first entering this world.

Daily Reflections

What we have been is an established
and unchangeable fact.
What we can yet become is an unlimited
boundless opportunity.

~

Break off the "rear-view mirror" and
concentrate upon what lies ahead.

There is little difference between one who has given up his life and one who has given up his hope.

Daily Reflections

Eating alone is better than mingling
with those whose conversation
is negative.

Stand guard at the doorway of your mind.

What we become largely determines the kind of people, events, books, and lifestyle that we select.

Determination to change can be like a mental elevator ride. We move ourselves upward with our thoughts and actions but some thoughtless person keeps pushing the "down button".

~

It is our natural destiny to grow, to succeed, to prosper, and to find happiness while we are here.

The only limitation on our abilities is our inability to easily recognise our unlimited nature.

Daily Reflections

Attitude determines choice, and choice determines results.

Daily Reflections

All that we are, and all that we can become, has indeed been left unto us.

◡

In the cycles and seasons of life, attitude is everything!

Daily Reflections

Experience the changing of life's cycles without being changed by them.

Do ordinary things - extraordinarily.

Take charge of your life.

~

The truth will set you free.

Formal education gets you a job.
Formal education can make you a living.
But Self education will make you a fortune.

Evaluate the past to set a better future.

Happiness is having values in balance.

Discipline is the foundation on which all success is built.

Remember: To make progress you
must actually get started.
Unless you change how you are - you'll
always have what you've got.

Daily Reflections

You never have a second chance to make a first impression.

Learn to express not impress.

Maintain your credibility.

As a parent, it's not what you do so much as what you become for your children.

Daily Reflections

Develop a working knowledge of life
and people.

A journal is a collection of the ideas
that make a difference to you.

Put more of yourself into what
you say.

Daily Reflections

Other books available from Brolga Publishing:

By E. James Rohn
Five Major Pieces To The Life Puzzle
The Seasons Of Life
Treasury Of Quotes
Seven Strategies For Wealth And Happiness

By Denis Waitley
Psychology Of Winning - Hard cover edition
Seeds Of Greatness - Hard cover edition
The Treasure Within

Any enquiries to:

Brolga Publishing Pty Ltd
C/o GPO Box 959, Ringwood, Victoria 3134, Australia.

Daily Reflections

THE SEMINAR COMPANY

AUSTRALIA'S LEADING PERSONAL DEVELOPMENT COMPANY

For further information on Australian Seminars

CALL 07 - 832 2155
1800 - 65 4488

Suite 2, 35 Astor Terrace,
Spring Hill, Queensland, Australia.